ARIES HOROSCOPE 2020

Aries Horoscope

2020

Copyright © 2019 Mystic Cat

All rights reserved. This book or any portion thereof may not be reproduced or used in any manner whatsoever without the express written permission of the publisher except for the use of brief quotations in a book review.

The information accessible from this book is for informational purposes only. None of the data within should be regarded as a promise of benefits, a claim of cures, a statutory warranty, or a guarantee of results to be achieved.

The images are used under license from Shutterstock, Dreamstime, or Deposit-photos.

Aries

Aries Dates: March 21 to April 19
Symbol: Ram
Element: Fire
Planet: Mars
House: First
Colors: Red, white

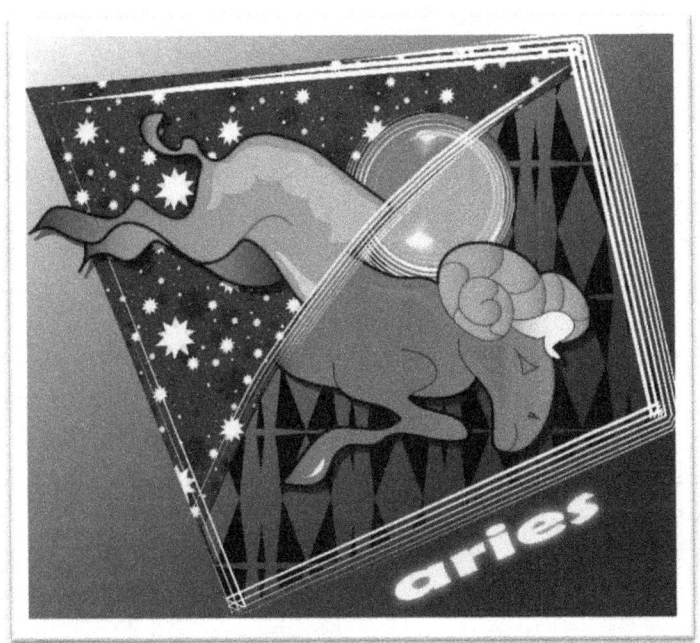

JANUARY HOROSCOPE

Astrological & Zodiac Energy

Visionary ~ Expressive ~ Innovative

Work & Career

You may have some limiting beliefs around success and abundance. If you're feeling stuck, look at your mindset, and find ways to broaden your perception. You are set to enter a cycle which brings good fortune into your world, it does draw the right type of people and brings you friendships which leave you feeling refreshed instead of drained. It does give your spirit a boost, and this encourages expansion. The winds of change are blowing into your life soon. It does involve a surprise or two, it has you feeling adventurous, and enables you to release an area which has been tightly bound up with your spirit. As you end one phase, a new area activates, receiving relevant information soon lays the groundwork for this journey to unfold. Your intuition plays a part in guiding you correctly, your creativity is also heightened. Something rare and beautiful coming into your world soon. It does offer an enticing path which leads to the development of a substantial goal. Your independent spirit relishes an environment which is progressive, innovative, and adventurous. You forge ahead and illuminate a situation which plays a prominent role in events on the horizon. It is a magical time to expand your life with new energy. Change is imminent, movement is your best option, focusing forward you can obtain fantastic progress on achieving long sought after goals. Your action-driven spirit is ready to finish this chapter and dive into a new area of growth. Tweaking your plans, streamlining your focus, brings you to a productive section where you can obtain incredible results.

Love & Romance

Singles this month hear news about someone who had fallen by the wayside. Hearing from this person satisfies your curiosity, it gives you peace of mind and enables you to put the situation to rest. It does bring a slower pace into your world, you begin to set the boundaries required to navigate an emotional chapter, which sees you untangle sensitive areas, and create space for a new world of potential to flow into your life soon after. It sets the stage for a chapter where you can untangle a mystery from the past. You navigate the nuances of a previous episode, it gives you a good outlet where you can clear the air with one person in particular. This nurtures a situation and helps you get closer, going more profound, and resolving the past. Revisiting this time proves to be fruitful, unlocking the dynamics with someone meaningful. You are transitioning to a new chapter, it does create a wonderful time of new potential. You are ready to move forward and get involved with a person who matches your energy. Things may have been stalling recently, that's just a sign of changing things up and re-energize your focus on a path which offers valuable dividends.

Couples this month find that patience and flexibility are rewarded with a closer bond. This person is drawn to your compassionate nature, they feel you share something special. This one is motivated to organize their life in such a way that things can unfold more securely. This person does find this connection is magnetic, it's difficult to reconcile the sensitive feelings it brings into their life. This person does question and doubt in their ability to keep the bond close, they have never felt this way for anyone else, you have made a lasting impact on them, and this continues to encourage them to focus on smoothing out rough edges and deepening the potential possible with you. This person has been feeling under pressure, work is causing a strain on their spirit. This one feels they have a lot to accomplish and worries that efforts may not be up to standard. They do want to make your priority, but they need more balance in life before this person can build a better connection with you. It does show that this individual cares very much about the relationship, and their efforts are made to provide a stable environment for you both.

IDEAS & CREATIVITY

The path ahead clears, and you reveal an enticing vista of possibilities. This re-energizes, it motivates you to push back the boundaries and surround yourself with a supportive crew who understand and nurture your life. All in all, it is a busy time, which ultimately provides you with a rich source of healing. As you travel down this road, you draw harmony, deepen your compassion, and heighten your empathy towards others. There is a powerful new option coming, which helps you transform your situation. This alignment refreshes the potential in your home life. It clears space where you can tap into creativity and get connected to innovative solutions. It does nurture home and family life, offering practical options which draw benefits into your world. It helps transition you to a happier chapter. You are set to achieve a more settled and stable environment. It does see incredible support flowing into your life from a departed loved one. Dreams are coming serendipitous signs and random events which all tally up as a beautiful show of support from the divine world. This rejuvenates and offers you a fresh start where you can feel more grounded and confident about expanding your life.

ISSUES & HURDLES

This month involves taking time to process the past. Contemplating your current situation, and envisioning your future aspirations, does set the stage for new ideas to enter your vision. It is a time of patience as you wait for further information to be revealed. It does offer you an excellent ripple effect of healing, which draws abundance into your world. Slowing down creates more freedom, this is true at this time. Focusing on nurturing your spirit is vital in creating a grounding effect, which nurtures and stabilizes your essence. Creating self-care rituals isn't a waste, it allows you to be creative, productive, and mindful. You are hard-working, resilient, and dedicated to improving your life. Taking time out is also an essential factor. Your life has been one of emotional highs, and lows. In this unpredictable terrain, there is fertile ground for self-development. Your flexibility and tenacity is a powerful tool you can use to improve your situation. The sun is set to enter your life soon, and this gives you an area to explore, which complements your skills, it offers you a great outlet for your talents. Wrapping up the energy which limits progress does kick off a new cycle of potential. Clearing the decks makes space for new options to arrive.

FEBRUARY HOROSCOPE

ASTROLOGICAL THEME & ZODIAC ENERGY

SUCCESSFUL ~ GUTSY ~ AMBITIOUS

WORK & CAREER

This is a month of practicalities, you get down to business, streamline and organize your life, letting you focus on the demands which rise to the top. It is a productive week, you grapple with areas that tend to fall by the wayside. Tidying up loose ends does create space for new ideas and inspiration to begin to sprout. It does see a more social vibe by the month's end, which offers you a fantastic escape from your everyday routine. You kick-off a fresh chapter of potential when news arrives to expand your horizons. It overhauls your lifestyle, you enter a time of manifesting excellent outcomes. This takes you to towards more significant endeavors, it does spotlight growing your situation, and taking on initiatives which connect with business-minded ideas. It re-fuels your tanks of inspiration and lets your mind run wild with new ideas. It is a busy time, which does enable you to make progress on your goals. This month is also a time of strength, a situation requires a choice is made. Utilizing courage, you exhibit strong leadership abilities. It does enable you to focus on building an area which offers the chance to change your environment for the better. There is much to look forward to, a new cycle of creative energy is at your disposal. It sparks a spontaneous and trailblazing time.

LOVE & ROMANCE

Singles discover a burst of inspiration arrives, which puts you on the path towards developing an area that sees you mingling with other people of a similar mindset. You discover a bond is possible with the one who blends their ideas and thoughts well, communication with this person flows smoothly. Conversations ahead continue to deepen the relationship, and this could turn into an exciting new connection for you to explore. A feeling of being comfortable and at home is a beautiful sign that things are finally flowing correctly for your personal life. It does give you insight into the path ahead, you discover opportunities arrive to help nurture this bond further. It is a path which illuminates abundance, joy, and kinship. A powerful moment forward brings you closer than ever to this person. There is potential brewing below the surface, this person does find you engaging, and is considering developing the situation further. It is likely to unfurl gently over time, and this creates stable foundations from which to progress a closer bond with this one.

Couples see that their partner begins to open up, it suggests that they no longer held back by fear, and begin to speak their most profound truth to you. This makes way for a new chapter which opens a gateway towards developing a closer bond. It could see things accelerating swiftly forward. You do benefit from the development of a soul bond. This represents a lofty pinnacle that you reach, it does bring blessings into your life. You head towards a productive chapter with one who is lively and brilliant. It sparks promising synergies where you can open your heart and share more profound thoughts with the one who gets you on a deeper level. This person helps you release the past and get you in touch with your true feelings. It does head to a chapter which offers joy, there are gains on all levels, which are both emotional and spiritual. This person paves the way for a beautiful time where they become more open in allowing the potential to flow into the situation. It does help them see clearly the best way to build those solid foundations which create a stable phase of growth. This leaves you feeling expansive about future potential.

IDEAS & CREATIVITY

During the February 9 Supermoon in Leo, you unwrap a cycle of new creative energy. It leads to a bold chapter where you embark on a journey which sparks a spontaneous adventure. There is plenty of wild and imaginative power at your disposal, it motivates and inspires your mind. You yield new opportunities, it does bring a fantastic journey into the light. Being discerning about which areas to develop helps you navigate the potential ahead easily. This is an excellent chance to rebrand your image and get involved with a new area which expands your skills. It grows your talents and harnesses an incredible creative force which offers you room to improve your life. It does help you pack in plenty of fun in an expressive chapter ahead. This is a time of impulsivity, new adventures, and incredible expansion. News arrives, which inspires and delights. It brings new energy, this heralds the start of a fresh chapter of potential. Soon enough, there are positive signs that your situation is evolving, taking you towards a stellar section which offers room to grow your dreams. As you peel back the layers of potential, you reveal a boost which broadens your perception and expands your life. This revolutionizes the potential possible and draws enthusiasm. Sudden changes bring new opportunities, it catapults you towards an active phase of growth. You harness your senses of vision and intuition to guide you towards learning new areas. This is fueled by a strong desire to better your circumstances, having faith in the outcomes possible, you leap forward, towards an exciting and adventurous area. It does give you a new perspective and sets the bar higher for what you can achieve. There is an impressive total of 4 supermoons in 2020. The more you tune into it, the more you are aware that you are going in the right direction. Radiating dynamically, you make headway on your goals. Your epiphanies are set to blossom under a promising sky.

Issues & Hurdles

Healing this month is about reestablishing emotional balance. It creates a stable platform from which to grow your spirit. Blocks, limitations, and hurdles can create an energetic burden which weighs down the potential possible. Engaging in a practice which nurtures yourself, does help create space for wellness and abundance to blossom. Being mindful, practicing a therapeutic modality helps grow your gifts. Yoga and meditation are just two examples. This month speaks of slowing down and savoring the weeks ahead. It's time to enjoy and spend time with friends and areas that you value. It does shine a spotlight on your closest bonds, nurturing the ties that bind, draws, wellness, and abundance into your life. There is someone who plays a significant role in the chapter head, connecting and sharing conversations with this person is on the stars. Your strength, wisdom, and insight are called upon by someone who shares their problems with you. Your generous spirit helps this person find a solution. It is also a reflective phase, which may see you processing complicated feelings, and creating space to resolve an area which has left you feeling conflicted recently. It is a time, which can leave you feeling frayed, some misunderstandings may bring complications. It does trigger your sensitivities, stepping back, being mindful, helps deflect energy which could leave you feeling frustrated or out of sorts. By month's end, you draw harmony into your life and spend time with people who leave you feeling refreshed. It can rejuvenate and improve your mood as they are on the same wavelength.

MARCH HOROSCOPE

ASTROLOGICAL THEME & ZODIAC ENERGY

PERSISTENT ~ TENACIOUS ~ CONSTRUCTIVE

WORK & CAREER

You get off to a productive start, and this leads to a busy time, it does see headway occurring around some of your larger goals. Things don't land in your lap without the effort being expended to make things happen. It is a highly creative chapter which sees you operating efficiently and at an energetic level. It does let you dive in and create a bounty which can be harvested over the subsequent phase. This is a great time which offers you a fresh start, an opportunity crops up which entices you to create space for something new to be developed. It provides a boost and kicks off a fantastic new phase. It does focus your energy on reaching your goals, prioritizing and streamlining does see you create a channel which offers you expansion and growth. You are ready to put the finishing touches on expanding your situation and reach for a new goal. It does take you on a path of progression, this potential ripples across your life and leads to a trail which sparks areas of interest, it does see you growing your vision, and this gives you the green light to use your creativity to stunning effect. Your unique gifts flourish under an auspicious sky. There is an area of interest which hits a high note with you soon. It is an expressive time which offers you an incredible ability to develop a space which shifts your focus forward. This horizon-broadening chapter grabs your attention, it lifts your spirits, and tempts you to broaden your scope. It does see you reaching for a goal which is more significant, brighter, and more exciting. It launches your potential to the stratosphere.

LOVE & ROMANCE

Singles discover an opportunity ahead provides the right terrain to connect with someone who plays a significant role in future events. Crossing the path of this individual does bring you an incredible breakthrough, it takes you towards a chapter which offers you a chance to develop a meaningful bond. It's a time of expansion and adventure, it's going to see fantastic progress occurring which is in alignment with your vision. This is a time which brings lovely community activities to light. You may discover several social opportunities swirling around, tempting you to mingle and spend time with others. It does create magic, it guides you towards an enchanting, social environment. The future spotlights a time of potential, it does see a bond developing and becoming more intimate. This brings a critical turning point, it leads to an emotional time of revealing deeper feelings, and this triggers an active phase of growth. It is an especially sensitive time, focusing your thoughts on where you want to head does help set the right tone to make things come together with intention.

Couples reveal it is a time of deepening interpersonal bonds and beginning to get a feel for future possibilities. This is someone who offers you plenty of support, and it does bring new ideas and inspiration to light. This person feels the situation is unfolding gently over time, there are good signs that it is going to move into new territory soon, bringing with it a more stable basis for future growth. However, it is a situation which has taken this person out of their comfort zone, this takes a little time for them to integrate their deepening feelings for you, it is creating a stable environment which offers a firm foundation from which to launch an excellent chapter of potential from. There are indications that this is going to move into something more official soon, and this does see you celebrating an unusual shift forward. It is a lovely time which hits a high note, it considers an incredible path of abundance open. This person has broadened your horizons, and they lift your spirits, running the right music for your life. It is a bond which brings new heights and kicks off a chapter of planning for future growth. It's a time of inspiration, this person is highly motivated to create a bond which offers room to blossom.

IDEAS & CREATIVITY

You may be feeling ready to shift gears and forge a new path which offers you creative expression. You may discover an area which brings new opportunities, it gives you a chance to take your artistic gifts to a new level. You have unusual talents, and there are going to be some attractive options for reaching you soon to progress your goals. You have fantastic gifts, and your unique flare put you in the box seat to manifest an area which offers robust potential. It does guide you towards an auspicious area, your imagination comes up with some fantastic ideas, making the most of your creative concepts. You enter a dynamic time, it attracts support from others who are well connected and able to offer a lending hand. This is a time where you can draw new options, which give you an outlet for any nervous energy. If you have found yourself feeling distracted recently, finding an area which captures your interest, will help focus your creativity and see you regain a shift forward. It draws abundance into your life and provides you with an area you can progress further. This is a time of new beginnings and fresh starts. It does attract your attention and fans the flames of your creativity. A dream opportunity could arise, this sees you make speedy progress, your creative talents are expressed with a unique flair. It does bring more motivation to expand your horizons and touch you down in an inspiring new area. A breakthrough is arriving to snap you out of your recent hibernation.

Issues & Hurdles

You are someone who can overcome hurdles and deal with life's problems succinctly. This is the time where it is beneficial to pause and take stock of your situation, you see clearly the past and the issues which hindered your progress. The essence of carrying inventory is to rebalance your energy and create space for the new potential to blossom. Restoring equilibrium does see growth ahead, it gives you a deep emotional awareness, and leads to the development of a situation which captures your interest. This sees you making strides forward. You may feel lost at times, too many demands on your energy create a sense of chaos. Finding ways to ground your spirit does draw balance, it expands your life and restores equilibrium. Evaluating larger goals highlights new options you can explore. You have unique gifts to share with a broader audience. You have a struggled with change recently, but you are gifted with both perseverance and determination. Though you have experienced setbacks, you are set to reveal new areas which offer you more joy and happiness. Living a life of purpose is the first step in healing those parts of your spirit, which have felt weary. You are on the road to finding your right path, this takes you on a journey of self-discovery. You may be feeling restless, there is a great deal of activity simmering below the surface, this relates to being in the box seat to grow your potential. You discover a journey of growth and learning beckons, this helps you capitalize on your gifts, it takes you towards the path which offers terrific expansion. Exploring a broader range of options does bring incredible change, and illuminates an opportunity which propels you towards a journey of promise.

APRIL HOROSCOPE

ASTROLOGICAL THEME & ZODIAC ENERGY

EXPANSIVE ~ IMAGINATIVE ~ CURIOUS

WORK & CAREER

It is a month which offers a whirlwind of activity, you develop an area which offers room for progression. Your centered and purposeful energy delights in having the right outlet to grow. Tangible feedback provides you with acknowledgment, it reinforces your sense of self and helps you feel confident that you are on the right track. It is a stabilizing force, and this provides you with a secure foundation from which to grow your dreams. It sees a powerful shift occurring which take you towards a landscape filled with harmony. Friendships bloom, issues with communication clear, and you see vital signs that the storms you have weathered are now dissipating. It does bring your mojo back and has you feeling energized about improving your life. You may even take on a larger goal and feel confident about your ability to see it through to its final destination. You tune into an area which is practical, productive, and gives you room to progress your situation. There is plenty of blessings to be grateful for soon, it is a lucky time, and this revitalizes and restores your spirit. In fact, you may land an exciting offer, and this gives you the ability to change your trajectory should you decide to head down a path which diverges from your everyday circumstances. Looking at your life and where you need to head next, you are likely to score a significant epiphany, which helps you change what is required to shift to progress your goals. It does send a surge of revitalizing energy, your confidence is on the rise, and you feel proactive about creating robust growth. This marks a turning point, it's a time where you decide to develop your talents and take things to the next level. A surprise crops up which offers you an advantage. This has you sashay through the month ahead with a lighter step. You have journeyed through a time of closure, healing, and resolving outworn energy. This created the space needed to replenish and restore your spirit. Once you discover the option ahead, you integrate growth and expansion into your life again. This kicks off an incredible chapter of excitement and new adventures.

Love & Romance

If things have felt quiet on the romance front, you can expect a new flow of energy to sweep into this area to help shift things forward. It does lead to an expressive chapter that could bring a romantic boon into your life. This begins a time of breakthroughs, it does allow more open and authentic communication to flow into your world. Knowing where you are headed with your personal life, creates the security you have been hoping for. A new beginning is marked for you. Releasing outworn energy does open the door to a brighter future. It is an essential emotional crossroads, focusing on compassion does help ease the sense of upheaval which has been around your life. It signifies powerful healing is possible, you can turn this around and improve the situation, providing you with tangible results.

New prospects are arriving, this sees you embrace a chapter which offers you the chance to reinvent yourself. It does create a beautiful shift to a route which is ripe for expansion. It has you focus on lifestyle improvement and building areas which draw passion and joy into your world. It does give you the green light to take a leap of faith and begin a fresh start. A surprise arrives at lightning speed soon. This could revolutionize your potential, and enable you to make things happen with a bold flourish. Putting a splashy mark on your life, it resets your potential, it sees you primed to enjoy an excellent, vibrant chapter which is dynamic and eventful. It squarely puts you in the box seat to develop your life and embrace a happy chapter which brings you advancement. You can use this outgoing energy to increase your social circle, it takes you towards new friendships and group activities which add more spice to your life. It may also see you reconnecting with those you haven't seen recently, expanding your social aspect draws abundance into your life. It is an especially important factor in creating a stable and supportive foundation. There are opportunities ahead to mingle, and this kicks off a joyful time.

Couples may find that their partner has been under pressure, the demands on their time have made it difficult for them to spend quality time on the situation. Things improve in the chapter ahead, this person can lessen their workload, and this enables them to build a better bridge of communication. This situation will ripen over the fullness of time. This individual does need time to think about values, the direction they want to go in, and then needs to streamline their situation and create enough space for things to unfold in a more manageable fashion. This person is focusing on improving the stability in their life, they are taking steps which are practical and grounded. They want to stay flexible and adaptable and be able to weather any bumps without feeling emotionally sensitive in the future. Things will become more balanced, time shared together lead to conversations which are more open and authentic. It sets the stage for a closer bond to flourish, high seeds have been planted, and this is likely to grow if nourished. This is a situation which unfolds gently over time. Communication may have been problematic, but inspiration is coming, which enables further bonds to be developed. It is a situation which leads you out of your comfort zone, it removes self-imposed limitations. The energy is simmering below the surface, there is a beautiful bond emerging. It does see a closer situation is possible. Nurturing this connection leads to a more intimate chapter with this person. Your love interest does see you as someone creative, expressive, and optimistic. This person does see you as someone they can depend on. This person appreciates your loyalty and ability to offer practical advice. They may have a tendency to take you for granted, and this can make them complacent. This one needs to lift their game if they want to make the most of things. It does suggest that serious bonding is ahead, this person is looking for the right outlet to nurture this situation further. It does take them out of their comfort zone, and this has made them put the brakes on recently, as they do get nervous.

IDEAS & CREATIVITY

The April 8 Supermoon in Libra takes you to a transformation which is profound and healing, this highlights a radical change which guides you towards becoming your highest potential. It kicks off a time of new possibility. This helps you improve your home situation, there are some strategic moves which are made to release the demands which drain your energy. It does enable you to enter a time of rejuvenation, you kick back, and relax with kindred spirits. It's also an excellent time to take stock of your goals, recommitting to achieving a dream does see you finish strong and bold. It is a time which bestows the blessings of luck and fortune upon your shoulders. This lightens your load and enables you to head towards a route which offers growth and expansion, this abundant pathway has been evolving for some time, and it unveils a new level of potential soon. This kicks off a cycle which integrates the development of some impressive goals and dreams. It does give your life an incredible boost. Unexpected changes, land in your lap like a windfall from the heavens. It is a surprise bonus and does see you taking a measured risk to put yourself out in a phase of expansion. Pushing back the boundaries of your life does improve your confidence. Your sense of self-worth is on the rise, and opportunities will emerge which provide you with an outlet for your restless energy. In fact, you attract a fantastic prospect soon. You will find more of these exciting discoveries as you tune into your intuition and messages from above. Opportunities are coming, which help you develop your talents, you have spiritual gifts, and these are set to evolve, it could really turn into a concrete path for you to explore, but you won't know unless you continue to grow this area.

Issues & Hurdles

The Supermoon in Libra this month provides you with a prime time to release the past, letting go of resentments and frustrations resolves areas which have been holding you back. If you have found your creativity has been suppressed, this is a sure sign that inner work is necessary. Creating a space to nurture your spirit brings positive vibrations into play. You soon ring in a chapter which sees harmony restored, what may have been challenging the cycle makes way for new growth. You are wise to be guarded and careful about re-establishing a situation with a person from your past. It has been a difficult time where you learned some tough lessons, but there is potential for a reconnection to emerge, which enables you to resume forward momentum with this individual. Taking it slowly begins a process of healing, more communication provides you with clarity, you'll start to get the clear answers needed about this option. Life gets more comfortable soon, you resume momentum, and this helps you gain traction on obtaining your goals. You begin to see the path clear, solutions and answers are found which enable you to progress.

All in all, you integrate the harsh lessons learned and come out the other side battle-worn yet willing to apply the knowledge acquired to obtain the highest result possible. It does set the scene for a productive phase of growth. You may have been through an unpredictable time recently. If you have faced a difficult situation which saw you reacting first and feeling volatile. You are set to resolve this situation, new energy is a brewing which enables better communication occurring. It does see you focusing on your closest ties, and this helps you not get caught up in the drama, it provides a stable basis from which to ground your energy.

MAY HOROSCOPE

ASTROLOGICAL THEME & ZODIAC ENERGY

EXPANSIVE ~ SPIRITED~ INVOLVED

WORK & CAREER

You get news about a deal soon, it sweeps in exciting potential and has you making a move towards developing an area of interest. If you have been exploring new options, you scope out a path which is right for progression. This touches your life with inspiration, you carve out a pretty significant area and make it your own. This brings change and good fortune. Life is about to become engaging, the pace picks up, there is activity coming, which is curious, and governs a more social environment. It does launch a new chapter around close bonds and friendships. Engaging conversations draw a meeting of the minds, it does have you exploring fresh ideas and innovative dialogues. Spending quality time with kindred spirits brings joy. You can sail through the chapter ahead, it is a voyage which highlights new adventures. Your wanderlust is driving you towards expansion. There are many possibilities which beckon and offer you a chance to branch out and discover new areas. Exploring your options do provide you with an enticing array of potential. It is a time of increasing self-expression and creativity. You are going through an active phase of growth, while you may be looking back to the past, you are in fact experiencing a powerful transition which takes your potential to a new level. You discover an area which is in alignment with your gifts, it shines a spotlight directly on developing your talents. This is a path which is ripe with inspiration and opportunity, it does have you feeling enthusiastic, and marks a turning point where you can achieve a breakthrough. You are traversing a time which draws stability and balance into your world. You score a debut where you can harness a creative aspect to full advantage. It does have you moving in alignment with your vision, and this enables you to slow down and appreciate the journey. You become more aware of what you are hoping to achieve. Changes are coming, you will feel it helps you to shine. An unscripted adventure awaits your open heart.

LOVE & ROMANCE

Singles may discover refreshing potential arrives late this month, there is a meeting which takes you by surprise, there is a connection of mind and spirit. Fascinating dialogues leave you feeling refreshed. This amps up the potential in your love life, it brings you clarity and abundantly impacts your life. It is a bond which has a robust interpersonal element, intimacy is rife, and the conversations shared activate broad perspectives which offer endless possibilities. Things come together for you soon. It does bring more communication and a sense of community into your world. Support is coming from a surprising ally. It does bring a long-overdue shift towards abundance and smooth sailing. There is also creative energy swirling around your vision, taking time to disconnect from distractions will help you tap into new ideas. You are someone who cherishes home life and believes in strong family ties. Your emotional foundations thrive when in a committed relationship. There is a turning point coming, which marks a transition towards a happy chapter, it gives you essential insight, allowing you to feel confident about developing a bond.

Couples this month find that there are opportunities to develop their romance. Further, it does pick up momentum, trust, and faith build stable foundations. This helps you take a leap of faith, and it inspires you to see the boundless possibilities which surround this relationship. It does fast track you to towards an abundant chapter where the sun sails into your world, and you can develop long term goals. It does see you step boldly into a more profound situation soon. There is a lot of potential emerging over the coming chapter. This situation evolves and deepens, long-term goals begin to take shape, and you gain clarity into where the bond is headed. This allows you to feel more secure and start to trust that this is a person who is capable of being there for you. There have been a few hurdles along the way, but it is worth being patient with this person as they do care a lot. It takes time to deepen the trust with this person, once they take a leap of faith, it does see a flurry of openhearted conversations this month build a stronger bond.

IDEAS & CREATIVITY

You are an inspiration to others. You can nurture bonds, and your sensibility does create a balance which smooths over conflict. However, those who stir up drama only drain your precious energy, distancing yourself from people who take advantage of your nature does help set appropriate boundaries. Nurturing your creativity is also essential, new options are arriving to tempt you towards growth and artistic expression. You are someone who has special talents to share. Your unique creative abilities are set to shine a light towards giving back and being of service. You can push for growth and expansion, your demanding attention to detail provides you with ample room to take your talents to a whole new level. A meticulous approach offers you a trajectory which leads to the stratosphere. There are attractive options ready to be revealed. You are prepared to put some of your visions into motion, it does see you structuring plans in the chapter ahead, and it this brings clarity around ambition, goals, and professional success. Your energy is focused on obtaining a workable plan, and sorting out your options helps you refine and choose wisely. Things are set to become active and busy for you. It does bring many changes to your life. Exciting developments are occurring around your life, which is connected with forms of communication. Writing, teaching, learning, or even publishing to a broader audience could be on the cards for you. You have creative talents currently underutilized, a more comprehensive and more involved journey does see you get connected with a worldwide audience.

ISSUES & HURDLES

The past has been an incredible time of learning, and this has strengthened your spirit as you have overcome many hurdles and come out the other side better for having made progress, even under challenging times. It does now take you to a crossroads, you have a chance to explore an area which offers you room to grow your vision further. It is a dreamy time of contemplating the path ahead, drawing abundance into your life. This is connected to energy, which is rising within, seeking a suitable outlet. Your creativity has been dampened by demands on your time and energy. This has led to an environment which bubbles with potential, yet you haven't been able to fully express your talents adequately. It's a clear sign that you need to create space to nurture your spirit and create an environment which is more conducive to personal growth. This is a mystical time which brings a spiritual element into your life. It does actually involve learning and activates a robust phase of personal growth. Your ability to manifest and improve your situation is evolving, this leads to a beautiful transformation, it sees a vision becoming a reality, and that gives you something to smile about. It is a time which nurtures emotional abundance. It shines a light on deepening a bond, and this highlights how important it is to build those deeper connections. It is a chapter which is expressive, it takes you out of your usual routine, and sees a better balance of work and play is achieved. You feel that you have a clear sense of the path ahead, and this gives you the freedom needed to expand those horizons. You reveal smooth sailing, it brings powerful insights which help you uncover new potential in your life. The important news is imminent, which provides you with a sign to head towards. Insight and clarity pave the way towards the direction explicitly meant for you. Once you see what is ahead, doubt is dissolved, this releases tension and beautifully aligns you with a shift forward. It does encourage you to take your potential to the next level.

JUNE HOROSCOPE

ASTROLOGICAL THEME & ZODIAC ENERGY

INTROSPECTIVE ~ HONORABLE ~ NOBLE

WORK & CAREER

Changes are coming, which give you a bevy of opportunities to explore. This pushes you out of your comfort zone, it does mark a time where you are moving in alignment with your spirit. These changes bring balance, they relieve the pressure and enable you to implement strategies which provide you with robust growth. It does help you make the most of new potential. You are set to enjoy an innovative and dynamic chapter, it gives you a chance to explore new avenues, it widens your perception, and draws exciting prospects into view. You can balance the demands on your time with your need for more freedom and self-expression. This enables growth, which is consistent, yet also draws you to areas which offer you a chance to grow your gifts. Expanding horizons leads to uncharted territory, brings a leap of faith, which shines a light on removing the boundaries which have limited progress. It is a boost which offers growth, adventure, and abundance. This sees a sense of reinvention arrive to usher in a chapter of change. It kicks off a time of new activities which lead to growth. It is a time of discovering your real ambitions, setting your gaze on a lofty target does set the tone for a specific vision to capture your interest. It is a career-driven time of expanding your options. Your professional plans are on track to climb further up the ladder soon. Your well-crafted ideas do provide you with an unexpected opportunity to increase your bottom line.

LOVE & ROMANCE

This is likely to be a focused, intense chapter for the single and looking Aries, it highlights an increasing sense of intimacy and emotional awareness. There is a lot to be revealed soon regarding relationship potential. You discover a situation blossoms with love and harmony. It helps you get back on course with your romantic goals. You find out that you can take this connection to a deep and permanent place, it allows you to explore synergies with one who offers you a great deal of support. This brings new potential into your world and leads to a happier chapter. This is a linking of minds, a sharing of kindred spirits. You both compliment each other in ways which bring out the best potential possible. It is a powerful message that this is someone who could impact you in positive ways, it may lead to a formal relationship. It does kick off a chapter where you can ramp-up the potential in your personal life, it resets your situation and helps you find your groove with someone special. The sunshine beams into your own life soon with a magnetic connection forming with an innovative and enticing individual. This is someone you can share openly with, you communicate well with this kindred spirit. Connecting with this prospective partner does see the magic emerge in your life. It leads to a time of bonding, as intimate thoughts are shared. It shines a light on security and new goals being possible.

Your personal situation may have hit a rough patch for the Aries in a romantic union, it does show you are in a cycle which does turn things down somewhat. This person has temporarily retreated to focus on other areas of their life. The good news is, it won't be long before you do see positive signs arriving. More open and transparent conversations lead to a rejuvenation of bonds. It is a time where you can recharge your spirit and think about the situation and the options available to you. More opportunities are coming into your personal life. If you have found, things have been restricted or stale, or recently, this is set to change. You can focus on developing goals which hold significant value to your life. This frees you from the sense of uncertainty you may have felt clinging to your energy. It is a time of excitement and surprises, a bond with another blends beautifully with your spirit. This person encourages you to step out of your comfort zone. There are opportunities to have a movement between you both which does feel flirtatious. The chemistry is simmering below the surface, this one is mindful of the restrictions which hold them back. It is an environment which does expand slowly, this person is supportive, and there is a sense that he is attracted to developing a closer bond. It is also balanced with the other areas of life, so you will not see any significant progress in the short term. There can be some challenges with this situation as there is a tendency to drift towards other areas which capture this one's attention. This can lead to anxiety as you may worry about the future and your inability to control where this bond is going. Self-doubt can cause isolation, barriers, and disenchantment. You inspire this person a great deal, and as the foundations continue to evolve, the bond proceeds to require maintenance.

IDEAS & CREATIVITY

You are on a journey which offers you room to grow your gifts. This is associated with a spiritual path, you have talents which could be shared with a broader audience. This takes you to a sector which draws abundance and provides you with a personal sanctuary where you can appreciate the blessings which surround your world. It does see your confidence growing, this leads to a more social environment which offers you room to forge new friendships. It is a valuable time where flexibility plays a role, this helps you make the most of a situation which shakes up your environment and progresses your talents to a new level of opportunity. This brings waves of change around your career path, it does offer you a chance to blossom and branch out in different areas. You excel at learning and growth during this productive aspect. It is a time of your groove and settling into a steady path of growth. It is a time of transformation, which alters your perception of what can be obtained. It does see you riding a roller coaster wave of emotions, unanticipated options strike a note, it gives you a broader sense of what can be achieved. This is a stellar time for expanding your horizons, opening your eyes to a new Vista. It gives you heightened activity, and in this productivity, you are in your zone. Thriving in busy environments, you take on the hectic pace, multitask as required, and diligently hit your mark. It does see improvement arriving, which gives you long-awaited answers. The feedback is positive, it starts a glorious chapter where you can structure more lofty goals, it's a golden phase for collaboration, joint ventures, and mingling with like-minded entrepreneurs.

ISSUES & HURDLES

There may be difficult energy intensifying around home and family this month, be aware that tension limits potential. If you feel stuck, spending time drawing in new areas can lift the lid on an exciting chapter of potential. It does light a path which offers abundance and gives you space to achieve your goals. You may just discover a dream flourishes while your attention is focused elsewhere. Exciting news could arrive by the months-end, things come together at long last. You have weathered some storms recently, but can now get ready for a revolution, a unique transition is coming, which sweeps in beautiful cleansing energy. It helps you heal, it leads you towards the advancement of expansion and freedom. You set your imagination on fire and rewrite the rules of your life to your own script. It does shake up your environment and tempts you towards change. While things have been complicated recently, an enticing twist occurs soon, forward motion is possible. In a surprise move, you discover a situation blossoms. This does highlight abundance which offers you a chance to grow your dreams. You may have had a few bumps in the road on the quest to develop your goals, but being adaptable and flexible does provide you with the highest outcome possible. You may have felt some turbulence from a rocky road recently, you are expanding your life and drawing a new chapter to life. This can feel like one step forward, two steps back, as you always need to re-evaluate and assess the path ahead and your chosen goals. You will find the right balance through pragmatic planning and lofty dreaming, your visionary ideas are guiding a shift forward.

JULY HOROSCOPE

ASTROLOGICAL THEME & ZODIAC ENERGY

ADVENTUROUS ~ ENERGETIC ~ VISIONARY

WORK & CAREER

You can expect developments in the area of business growth. As you map out new possibilities to explore, you mostly envision a trajectory which is more in alignment with your core goals. Enterprising and exciting options crop up to tempt you to branch out. You receive recognition for your talents and capture the attention of someone who seeks to open doors for you. This does help you develop your career to a higher level, this supporter feels you have impressive gifts that are currently underutilized. It does draw a path of abundance which places more security in your world, it brings a critical turning point for your work life. It is a time of change, there is plenty to be inspired by, you get your goals glowing with strong determination. It is a time which enables you to go broad and progress essential goals. Pushing your boundaries further does take you out of your comfort zone, yet it reveals opportunities which continue to motivate and inspire growth. It is opening a path which draws new options to light. A lot is happening in terms of communication and social choices, as well. You blaze through an uninterrupted time which sees you make progress on a personal dream. It does have you feeling positive about making those more considerable changes required to obtain your goals. You stake a claim on an area which feels meant to be, it does incredible spotlight potential which has you feeling excited and gives you plenty of inspiration to begin planning the steps needed to obtain your highest results.

LOVE & ROMANCE

Singles may You discover an area which entices you forward. It allows your personal life to be rebooted. As you head towards a bold chapter, you embrace the development of feelings with someone who captures your curiosity. There is a breakthrough around romance, creativity, and adventure. It launches you towards a phase which is a self-expressive, enticing, and emotionally rejuvenating. This does lift your spirits and enables you to dream big. This transition to a new chapter in your personal life may bring up old sensitivities. Your vision for the future is currently undergoing a time of change, you may find you alter or change the trajectory, this highlights the need to be flexible during this shift forward. As you navigate a unique environment with the utmost care, you find yourself in a landscape, which offers abundance earned through trust. The development of emotional bonds soon follows. The new potential around, love, creativity, friendship, and romance. It ignites powerful potential which enables you to team up with someone who inspires your heart. It does lead you to a turning point, one which offers you a path which is bold, expressive, and passionate. It could radically revamp your situation and take you towards an exciting adventure which offers long-term potential. This person draws lightness into your life. It is the silver lining in what has been a trying chapter. This one does make you smile with their colorful personality. It does drive a situation which is healing for you, and this sustains you during moments when you find yourself questioning the path ahead. It does encourage you to explore bold new terrain, giving yourself time to integrate and process heavy emotions maintains the sense of balance.

Those in a relationship reveal that they can expand the situation. It does bring an influence where you tune into your higher aspirations, it is a time of increasing clarity, your intuition is guiding you to develop a closer bond with the one who has captured your interest. It does seem that this is a situation which offers room to progress further. It is slowly unfolding, giving you time to assess progress, and move forward with a clear mind. This person becomes someone significant in your life, the situation eclipses all that has gone before, it revamps your options, and this sees you adopt a confident, new attitude. It is a bold time where you can transform your identity and forge a close bond. It does see you swimming freshwaters, and reaping the rewards of taking the time necessary to form a stable foundation with this individual. This sees you pursue goals of personal happiness and fulfillment. This person supports your ideas and enables you to grow and expand your life in a way which merges beautifully with theirs. It does have you thinking about long-term potential, you build things slowly, and with thoughtfulness. This is a factor in creating a bond that stands the test of time. You head towards a chapter which brings great joy into your life, it does see a situation deepening, you radiate prosperity with the one who is on a similar wavelength. Being with this person inspires and re-invigorates your spirit. It is a time which leads to meaningful moments and activities you treasure. Setting intentions at this time creates the right mind space to step forward into the next bold phase of life.

IDEAS & CREATIVITY

A moment of clarity provides a light bulb moment, it gives you insight into the path ahead, it provides you with new options. This has you feeling enthusiastic, it does enable you to channel higher energy, this magic courses through your life, it signifies a theme of improving circumstances, it allows you to access a path which is all about change and progress. Objectively identifying the correct way forward is an essential step in the right direction. This is a time where you can see impressive results in creating forward motion which propels you towards an exciting chapter. The pace may be hectic, it can even feel chaotic or unsettling. It does denote an active time of growth is indicated, this shifts your focus forward, it gives you the fuel needed to acquire positive change. Your innovative mind is ready to unleash fresh ideas and creative solutions. Life enters a fast-paced and exciting phase, there is a lot of newness coming, it does see you experimenting with different options to pick the one which offers the highest result. This dabbling with new areas is a process of refining and evolving your potential. It gives you a path which provides a potent brew of manifestation, and this sees you acquire new talents to add to your collection. You are in a time where significant changes are possible, it does see you reach a turning point, this may lead to an epiphany which provides you with a creative path that is begging to be explored. You make it your own personal mission to make sure things come together, having a clear incentive gives you the motivation required to focus your energy on achieving the highest result. This proactive energy is a big part of the changes ahead.

ISSUES & HURDLES

You may find yourself continually sacrificing parts of your spirit to placate and maintain a demanding environment. This challenges your ability to freely express yourself and feel content and happy. It is a bumpy ride, and it will continue to see you looking at the larger picture, and work towards obtaining a happy balance. It is a time which does offer you a variety of options, and this can make it feel difficult to know which path to head towards. I do see game-changing options arriving which give you clarity, this brings you the inside knowledge needed to know you are making the right choice. It does see more faith occurring, this opens the channels to a happier chapter emerging. You can progress your personal goals by focusing on and maintaining steady progress. You in a time of transition, this can feel unsettling, you are set to land in a new area of potential soon. It draws balance into your life, it allows you to see a path which offers you room to explore your passions. You scope out new options, which leave you feeling inspired. This enthusiasm shines a light on what is possible with the right mindset. Being flexible in your mindset opens the floodgates to a new flow of abundance. This is a phase which represents yourself, your dreams, desires, and personal goals. It is an emotional time where you slow down and integrate recent changes into your life. It may see you backtrack, looking at the past, and absorbing and reflecting on energy which has been pushed to the side. Now you have a chance to do inner work, reflect on where you have been, and where you are headed next. You have been through an unsettling time where there have been many rapid changes, things are now directed towards a new path, it does bring you enticing options. Reaching a turning point has you releasing the hold that the past has on you, and this allows you to create space for releasing all that stands in the way between you and your happiness. You are set to blaze through a time which is more self-expressive, and joyful.

AUGUST HOROSCOPE

ASTROLOGICAL THEME & ZODIAC ENERGY

IDEALISTIC ~ CONSTANT ~ THOROUGH

WORK & CAREER

This month sees you apply yourself diligently to the tasks at hand. You are organized, structured, and successful in your endeavors at work. Your personal strength is how you organize and plan. By creating the right structure and balance at work, you achieve an environment that is consistent, reliable, and productive. It provides the right foundations that establish heightened stability and future growth for you in your career. You express the energy of fire at work, you radiate warmth and steely determination. You provide sustenance to others, infusing your workplace with positivity, vigor, and vitality. You follow a straightforward path and use a no-nonsense course of action which allows you to achieve your goals. You are competent at work, with a down to earth attitude, which helps your energy to stay grounded during hectic times. You are skilled in many practical abilities, and overcome problems with a pragmatic approach. You are solidly grounded, yet creatively free and original. This blending of opposites and blurring of boundaries is prevalent around your energy this month. By understanding your inner workings, you utilize your most considerable skills and focus your concentration on the task at hand. Your consistent approach provides you with a sense of purposefulness and allows you to achieve heightened productivity.

LOVE & ROMANCE

Singles enjoy some changes which are arriving in your personal life. You feel excited about events on the horizon, you are ready to explore your options. It does lead to discovering a bond is possible with the one who is embracingly honest, this is someone who doesn't shy away from difficult conversations. They have a powerful intellect and feel a strong compulsion to speak their mind and tell you about their attraction. New energy reveals enticing options are available, you deepen a bond with one who is charismatic, and intelligent. Building a situation with this person takes the main focus in your life, it gets you in sync with developing a bond which makes your heart sing. It is a situation where you both connect well, perfect timing allows this situation to move forward and grow into something meaningful. You discover a condition which can be resolved through better communication. You strike a balance between progress and adaptability, it kicks off a chapter which draws abundance and leads to more intimacy in your personal life. A simmering attraction may ignite over the coming weeks, it emphasizes a bond which offers room to progress further. Deepening this situation does bring a surge of optimism and confidence that things are on the upswing. When you think back to the past, you see yourself as someone completely different than the person you are today. This shows how you have grown, and you are set to enjoy more self-development, which leads to an expressive chapter, you see an increase in confidence, this enables you to fearlessly speak your truth. It may also herald a time of igniting potential in your love life.

Couples; you have merged your life with the one who inspired change. You plunge into a beautiful adventure of developing emotions with someone who delivers a big eureka moment into your life. As you unveil the potential possible, you do begin to see long-term plans taking shape. Everything seems likely with this person. A romantic situation tugs at your heartstrings. It ignites an adventurous chapter which sizzles with potential. The chemistry with this individual is enticing. This person is proactive, they know what they want, you inspire them, and they are ready to tempt you forward. You feel encouraged to move past your comfort zone and explore the bountiful potential with one who lures you towards change. There may be a need to process heavy emotions to clear space for something new. Surprise news arrives to unveil something special. It makes way for a considerably lighter chapter, you have pushed through difficult circumstances and can embrace that feeling of being able to complete those hard-won victories. You find the situation which has been concerning you does undergo its next evolution, this sees a problematic area become more amicable. It does also provide you with expansion in your personal life. Something new is brewing, which entices you forward.

IDEAS & CREATIVITY

You radiate creative energy this month, this results in dazzling inspiration and creative brilliance. It indeed ignites a passion within you and propels you forward towards your goals with accuracy and confidence. You set your plans in place with a keen sense of purpose and are intensely creative as you harness a dynamic, and a pioneering spirit. This allows you to access the energy of manifestation, you radiate the positive power of the Aries star signs fire element, and this increases your vitality with determination, which allows you to propel you forward. Goals and aspirations planned for or set in motion this month bloom successfully, and soon become ready for further development. Your imagination is a source of inspiration and enthusiasm. As you gaze upon the potential possible in your life, you are drawn towards its promise of freedom, magic, and enchantment. You feel blessed by the artistic and creative thoughts, which entice you towards creative ingenuity, and self-expression. Your forward-thinking vision allows you a broad overview of the landscape ahead and offers you radiant, innovative solutions. You are being aided by the law of attraction to find creative solutions. You can feel that all things are now possible. This is a month of radiant and captivating thought processes. You think creatively rejuvenated, with your mind filled with new passions to develop.

ISSUES & HURDLES

A significant change is indicated, tearing down old layers which no longer serve your purpose, enables you to form a new foundation. This is a time of transformation and change in your life, as it is a month of conclusions and transformation. This points towards a great ending taking place in your life that initiates a new beginning occurs. These changes can be unsettling, and there is a need to maintain flexibility as you move from one life phase to the next. Change is necessary as you overcome hurdles and prepare to enter the next primary stage of your life cycle. This month represents a significant transition, as one aspect of life ends, and a new beginning is established. Do not fear change because it is in truth, only a transformation which will allow further growth and expansion to take place in your life. This is a month in which you feel the need to find focus and clarity in their life so you can regain lost ground. There is also a need to recognize and understand all elements involved in your personal hurdles. You are guided towards using your powers of reasoning and intellectual insight to see into the heart of the matter. This is a month in which you engage in authoritative personal assessment, in a search for truth, as you feel a need to discover the hidden elements involved below the surface. Powerful mental forces are utilized to cut away from wrong thinking and entanglements of the mind. This is the perfect month to cut away from old patterns of behavior, and start afresh with clarity and resolve.

SEPTEMBER HOROSCOPE

Astrological Theme & Zodiac Energy

Active ~ Perceptive ~ Original

Work & Career

You are rewarded with a new chapter which leaves you feeling energized and eager to start expanding your goals, you explore a new vision of potential. You are doing your best to carve out time where you can express your individuality, and engage in creative thinking. It's a chapter where you may diverge from your current role, and explore other areas which inspire your mind. It ushers in a time of creativity, drawing abundance into your world. You are finishing up a larger cycle of growth, you now tune in to your spirit, moving in alignment with your core beliefs. It denotes a spiritual journey which takes you to a new level of awareness. You currently have gifts and talents that have never been used. If you don't begin on this path, you will never truly understand what you are capable of. It does bring you to a vast and expansive arena of potential. A shift of potential takes you forward, it does turn in to a new vista which is filled with opportunities to share your vision with a broader audience. It gives your dreams a fantastic launchpad, this offers you the chance to harness your creativity, and embark on a trailblazing journey of self-development. It brings your ideas to the forefront of your awareness so that you can plan a path to obtain those meaningful goals. You are ready for a new journey, it does bring opportunities to team up with your favorite crew of innovators. This is also social time, you expand your circle, it sets positive outcomes in motion. The wheel is turning, you are ready to start a chapter which enables you to make essential changes. It emphasizes going after your dreams and creating lifestyle changes which take you to an expansive and adventurous phase of life.

Love & Romance

The Aries, who is single and looking for love, discovers that their social life is going to be a source of vibrant and dynamic elements in the chapter ahead. This is a fast-paced environment which is currently evolving, it draws new friendships to light, and may also include discarding those who don't respect your boundaries. If someone is ungracious and self-centered, your energy doesn't need that drama. It is a process of refining and drawing the right people into your world who nurture your spirit. You enter a bright time, which is more expressive and focuses on expansion and abundance. It does hit a passionate note in your life, it improves all areas, everything from romance to confidence, and self-expression. Under the influence of this robust environment, you discover the person who inspires and adds magic into your life. You are ready for a fresh start, a romantic interest sparks to life, leaving you feeling inspired. You are prepared to set the next time ablaze with new endeavors. It does see you making a bold statement, your confidence is heightened, this more positive outlook draws the attention of another. It highlights an enchanting chapter which sets the stage for a dreamy time of developing a meaningful bond. If you place your sights on your dreams, this focus is instrumental in harnessing the energy of manifestation. Things heat up for you soon, it does see you stirring a blend of powerful options, and developing a situation with an enticing love interest. It enables you to settle into a position which gives you an all-clear signal to head towards growth. This shifts your focus on your personal life, you hit your stride, and infuse your life with new dreams and goals. It does shine a light on what is possible when you expand your comfort zone.

For the Aries who is in a relationship; your love interest sees you as insightful, perceptive, and intriguing. This person may not feel able to fully open themselves to the situation. There is a sense of restriction which limits progress, this one doubts in their ability to deepen the bond this month. They wait for the time to feel right before exploring the synergy. Further, there is a sense that they think the relationship will develop naturally over time. This person wants to be a part of your life, and cultivating a bond and sharing experiences together does guide them towards a closer bond. Being flexible with them provides you with the gateway towards a happier chapter. You can create a sustainable path forward with them, which also enables you to maintain a sense of independence and freedom. It is a passage towards a new chapter of potential. Some lovely changes are coming, which allow you to enter a bountiful time, it does see growth with another, and this provides you with a wonderful sense of excitement. It creates a gateway from which something unique blossoms over the coming chapter. Life is aligning favorably for you, as your personal life improves, your heart ablaze with fresh inspiration. This situation is dynamic, fast-moving, and exciting. This person does feel positive about a shift towards developing a more meaningful bond with you. It is guiding them to explore this potential further and create space for future growth with you. This individual feels that you express a unique combination of openness and authenticity. They see you as someone who brings a great sense of fun and adventure into their life. It offers a vast array of possibilities which ignite a spark of happiness in their mind.

IDEAS & CREATIVITY

This is a curious time, it does not follow a linear path, so you can embrace a time which is adventurous, and has a tendency to bring unexpected news. Staying flexible with your plans, enable you to make the most of this expansive and lucky chapter. It amplifies your confidence, creativity, and self-expression. This translates to an authoritative time where you can manifest incredible advancement. There is a lot of potential coming which pushes you towards a time of expansion, and growth. It does see you moving towards developing bigger goals, and this may also include new friendships which shine a light on abundance and happiness. You may discover sparks of attraction that border on infatuation. This does capture your interest and gives you an overwhelming sense of excitement to ponder. A lighter chapter is arriving. It does see communication flowing freely, this gives you an excellent chance to catch up with those in your broader social circle. Your event planner is going to come in handy, as invitations crop up, which require attention to detail. Spending time with a gathering of friends, you discover there is plenty to celebrate in the chapter ahead. It is an especially heartwarming time which draws abundance. You reveal that opportunities are coming to support your dreams. It does prompt you to become more proactive about developing your goals. It has you feeling confident about exploring your options. It is an incredibly self-expressive chapter, you focus on personal dreams, and this highlights a fantastic pinnacle which may be reached through your perseverance and dedication towards taking action on your own behalf.

ISSUES & HURDLES

It is time to resolve areas which have limited your energy recently. This may involve some forgiveness work, you release the stress, and enter a phase of rejuvenation. Choosing to nurture your spirit does bring the space needed to embrace a path of renewal. It gives a soothing outlet for your soul, dials down the tension, enabling you to focus on wellness and healing old blocks.

Understanding the issues which trigger your sensitivities does provide you with a sense of being forewarned. It helps you maintain balance whenever you do happen to feel under fire. This is pivotal in creating the right kind of environment to fully thrive. Nurturing your spirit reconnects you to your true creative nature. It brings out the best in your potential. It does draw abundance and blessings into your world. You catch a lucky break soon when an area crops up which captures your interest. This is bringing new options into your life, you will have plenty to be grateful for, as it provides you with the wow factor. It is a lucky time with energy which revitalizes and leaves you feeling optimistic. This is drawing transformation and happiness into your life so that you can heal the past and embrace the future. There are some beautiful changes are coming around home and family. You go into things with a clear head, it enables you to take care of business, and get your goals in motion. A new phase is underway, and this brings your potential up a notch. Little goes under the radar, you spot an opportunity which feels like the right fit for your situation. It does enable you to create more considerable changes around your lofty goals.

OCTOBER HOROSCOPE

ASTROLOGICAL THEME & ZODIAC ENERGY

CAREFUL ~ OBSERVANT ~ AWARE*DONE*

WORK & CAREER

You have the magic touch at work, this leads to increased prosperity, security, and good fortune. You feel pride and a sense of achievement as goals are met, and journeys are completed. Your workplace position is secure, and you are building a firm foundation for future progress. This month epitomizes long-term security and contentment, your efforts at work are leading towards promotion, growth, and protection. This allows you to feel a sense of completeness, as all elements are working together in symbiosis. The positive outlook this month also refers to a state of an inner abundance, as you enjoy and appreciate your working life, it enriches your emotional state. This attitude of gratitude increases the capacity for attracting wealth into your life. Remember to pay it forward, as the more you share, the more you will be nourished by the richness of giving. This, in turn, attracts more abundance to you harness the law of attraction, and you reap the reward of positive Karmic flow. This also represents a time of completion for you. You will be rewarded with deep satisfaction and sense of stability as a major project is finished A fresh start on a new project at work inspires growth and leaves you feeling elated. Your adventure awaits, and it is the perfect energy to flame your passion and capture your imagination. You are successful in your latest endeavor and now are ready to set your sights on a fresh vision. Your imagination draws creativity, growth, and opportunity to you. Endless possibilities abound, as you are, indeed the true master of your destiny.

LOVE & ROMANCE

Singles discover that offer crosses your path, which provides you with a beneficial option. This brings substance and joy into your world, it brings you goals you can plan towards, it may change your priorities, as you shift your attention onto an area previously undiscovered. Being willing to open your mind, does advance your potential, it brings you on a new journey of discovery, which is exciting and adventurous. You discover your fortune favors bold moves, it is an auspicious chapter, a great time to expand horizons and dive into a more social aspect. As complications fade away, outworn energy dissolves, bringing you sunshine. An opportunity comes knocking, this sees your potential blossom over the coming months. A large social gathering is ahead providing you with a beautiful occasion, it brings a breakthrough which is a turning point. You lighten your load when an invitation crosses your path, which helps you harvest potential in ways which draw abundance. It does see the seeds you plant blossom into something significant. It takes you to a chapter which sees you becoming more social, and this connects you with others who share your values and ideas. It brings creative options to light, which give you an empowering sense of having the solutions needed to improve your situation. You are on the right path to living a life which resonates beautifully with your higher goals. You will soon be given more clarity about a new direction which draws joy. You are likely to attract several enticing options into your life soon.

The Aries in a relationship finds that the more you share with your love interest this month, the closer you become. It does offer you benefits on multiple levels, and you begin to get a sense of what is possible with this person. Someone has energy is entirely focused on you. It can feel overwhelming at times, as you try and find your way out of this maze, which has clouded your vision. You can progress while honoring the feelings in your heart. Taking time to explore fruitful dialogues leads to creating a sense of open transparency, which is needed to deepen a bond which can hold long-term prospects. This supports your vision for the future. You begin to see progress in a personal situation, things are moving forward, but it is not as fast as you would hope for. You may also find a new role on offer, one that requires learning, and it does open a new avenue for growth. It is a productive time which enables you to begin to see things take shape. This inspires your mind, and you contemplate future possibilities with a sense of hope and optimism in your spirit. A welcome surprise ahead draws the significant blessing into your world. It gives you a unique feeling of being appreciated by someone who captures your heart. It puts you in a position to plan long-term goals. Pausing to reflect on the abundance available in your home and family environment does strengthen your emotional foundations. A significant turning point brings refreshing news soon, which connects closely to your home life.

IDEAS & CREATIVITY

Opportunity favors the bold, you shine a light on new potential, you can expect the unexpected as there could be news which arrives swiftly to encourage you out of your comfort zone. Rapid, direct action sets in motion the events which propel you forwards and be prepared to strike with swift force as you harness the element of fire to reveal new options. This sudden burst of energy is symbolic of the intense heat and creative power contained within you. You will not let your progress be impeded by unnecessary hindrances that stifle your fiery energy. Expect full speed ahead as events rapidly occur in tune with high-velocity frequency this is around your potential this month. By adapting to this new frequency and rhythm, you give form to unique creative desires, and goals. This energy has arrived for this express purpose, and it allows you to process information quickly, and receive flashes of inspiration that dazzle you with increased potential. You use creative insight to forge new plans. This gives you the ability to delve into the yet unformed world and subtly weave threads of possibility into being. You take control of situations and use creative ingenuity, and manifestation to find solutions to problems as they arise. Your ability to manifest what you desire is high, and rather than over-intellectualize or overthink potential outcomes, allow yourself to let go and harness the essence of intuition. This will enable you to manifest the solutions needed in your life.

ISSUES & HURDLES

There is a need for increased vigilance and resilience this month. A secret is revealed in the form of a controversial message. You need to remain clear-sighted, insightful, and objective. Your integrity will allow you the skills required to settle this controversial news, and reestablish balance during a volatile situation. You play the part of a mediator and gracefully balance opposing forces. By exposing the truth, you right wrongs, and apparent confusion. Your clarity penetrates to the heart of the matter and cuts away all disruptive energy. This gossip and innuendo in but a hindrance on your path to your higher self, you move forward with sharp and clear insight, that clears the road ahead for all involved. It's essential to recognize that negative news or energy is subjective in nature, and does not necessarily reflect the actual circumstances of your situation. Do not allow this to disturb your peace, as it could lead to further unease, worry, and problematic emotions. Overcome this negative atmosphere by allowing yourself to be immune to the effects of other views and idle talk. This approach lets you see these issues as just mental static, and this helps you overcome a doubting or uncertain headspace so you can restore balance and harmony in your life.

NOVEMBER HOROSCOPE

ASTROLOGICAL THEME & ZODIAC ENERGY

SEASONED ~ ANALYTIC ~ POISED

WORK & CAREER

Focus and attention to detail will pay the most considerable dividends for your working environment this month. Utilizing your skills of craftsmanship and meticulous attention to detail, you cultivate professional excellence. You take pride in your work and achievements, and as you focus on each step of the journey with care and focused energy, you achieve a high degree of success. Wisdom and craftsmanship are required, as the pace is bold and you are under pressure to meet the demands of an increased world load. By applying a methodical approach, your discipline and diligence pay off. The progress is steady, but productivity is increased due to this being the busiest of months. Your inspiration, insight, and creativity come from a sensitive, intuitive place, this is a time of heightened artistic awareness, and you find yourself taking stock and redefining your working goals. You have accomplished a lot on your journey so far, yet there is much more that can be achieved. It is a month of golden ideas and creativity for you, and you will find that soul-searching results in a change of direction, and increased creative freedom. This leaves you feeling invigorated and revitalized by the months end. Embrace this divine creative energy that flows into your awareness, as it will help you achieve success in your life. There are also plenty of work politics and social events to navigate this month, brush up on your confidence and social skills, and you will shine, those who watch your progress will take note of your abilities.

LOVE & ROMANCE

Single and looking for love reveal an admirer this month, this person is connected to your more full social circle. An invitation/message arrives, which gets the ball rolling. You both attend the same event and share a discussion which sees the situation, click nicely. It does begin a path of getting to know each other better. There is significant potential with this one. It is a situation which shines a light on a romantic bond which is mysterious, magnetic, and magic. This is someone who inspires your mind, and it does blossom beautifully as you both are seeking similar things. You are drawing manifestation and abundance into your life. It does create a shift towards a powerful transition, it sees you embarking on a new adventure with someone who captures your interest soon. It leads to lively conversations, and a closer bond is formed.

The Aries in a relationship feels that there is a lot of potentials yet to be revealed with their love interest. Stability is the outcome of patience and flexibility. You draw abundance into your life, you can appreciate how far you have come on this journey. This person has a deeply romantic soul, they are compassionate and open to developing the situation further. This is a path which is built through sharing of experiences together, and opening the door to a happy life. This person has a wealth of knowledge to share with you. There is a deep desire to nurture and grow a bond which eclipses anything else you've ever had before. They are willing to open the door on a chapter which invites abundance into your life. There is a strong sense of wanting to protect you, and they do have the capacity to make things happen. It leads to a situation which offers robust potential, keeping flexible and open heightens potential.

IDEAS & CREATIVITY

This is a month where the wheels are turning in your mind, you see that it's time to plan for the future. The year is reaching closure soon, and with the beginning of a new year, just weeks away, it will be time to set in motion new plans, complete with new goals to be developed. It does open your creative awareness to a realm of possibilities. This creates a higher ceiling of potential, it is time to nurture those ideas in fertile ground. Personal growth is a significant aspect of your future journey, listening to your inner voice ignites your creativity, and nourishes your spirit, and takes you towards developing goals which are in alignment with your higher self. Doubt and anxiety are the niggling voice within you, which hold your real creativity back from reaching its full potential. Creating a harmonious environment, disconnecting from outward distractions such as social media, and areas which drain your energy is beneficial this month. It enables you to tap into the quiet voice within, it helps you dream up big ideas that you can start to grow and work towards. It is a mystical time, which is currently evolving and subject to change. Staying flexible and broadening the perception of what you are capable of will hold you in good stead during this time of planning for the future. Stability is available to you, you can certainly appreciate what your efforts this year have achieved. Your dreams are the essence of new inspiration which seeps into your fertile imagination, it's a timely chapter of planning for future growth.

ISSUES & HURDLES

As touched upon in the ideas and creativity section, doubt and anxiety are your biggest hurdles this month. It is time to release the fear, and take those leap of faith moves which guide you towards an expansive horizon where you can reach your true potential. Do the due diligence necessary, do your homework, don't be lazy this month. Make sure your plans, hold water, place appropriate safety nets in place when it comes to developing business ideas. This leads you towards robust growth, with an intelligent and pragmatic approach. This is about knowing you can reach for more and obtain stellar results, but there is not a magic wand that is just going to drop golden nuggets in your lap. You need to do the work necessary to achieve your goals. Keeping a journal, starting a vision board, having smaller steps to work towards, finding mentors that inspire you, keeping the right crew of people around your life, are all fantastic ways to increase your shift forwards. There are many ways to nurture your spirit and draw motivation into your life. Issues and hurdles only interfere with your life if you see them as barriers, the right mindset can overcome all limitations. The power of your mind is incredible, and tapping into that energy is fundamental in achieving Gold in all you do and all you resonate.

Additionally, this month does a set a tone of having to work more on interpersonal relationships, you are going to hear and see from more people over the coming weeks, and this can have you feeling out of your comfort zone. Create space to renew your spirit, and take time out from social activities if you find they impact your energy negatively.

DECEMBER HOROSCOPE

ASTROLOGICAL THEME & ZODIAC ENERGY

CHARMING ~ LIVELY ~ IRREPRESSIBLE

WORK & CAREER

This is a busy month, you are going to be put under the pump at work. It is a time where you go in strong, get the job done, and deal with a hectic pace utilizing your skills and harnessing a willingness to complete tasks and achieve powerful results. It is also month where you should remain open to new opportunities, you may be called to help out in other areas, this is a great way to learn and broaden the scope of your working expertise. It could even make way for new options to flow into your world next year. There is wonderful energy arriving this month, life is more social, invitations to mingle and share goodwill abound in the workplace. It does bring a happy tone, into play, life holds the promise of a brighter future, your action shapes your destiny. There is much to be achieved, and many blessings to appreciate this busy and active time. ,

LOVE & ROMANCE

The single Aries can enjoy the interest of one who sits just outside of your social circle. This individual is looking for ways to become closer and may choose a pathway which begins with an impromptu message. There is a positive vibe from this person that they are genuine, authentic, and hoping to build a bond which offers room for growth. This could be your ticket to an adventurous chapter of love and romance. You cross the path of someone flamboyant, romantic, and charismatic. It is a situation which takes time to fully unfold, but it does see creativity, self-expression, and harmony blossom. It's a new cycle which provides you with an enticing character to tempt you forward. This person is grounded in their relationships and does seek a bond which is purposeful, and meaningful. It brings advancement to your personal goals. Refreshing options are arriving for you. The tides turn in your favor, a spontaneous movement shared with another illuminates a more profound bond is possible. You discover this character is a better match for your situation. This is a person who is authentic and genuinely seeking a stable condition to develop, you have caught their attention, and things are set to come together with a flourish soon. Taking down your filters provides you with a glimpse of what might be. You are seeking a meaningful bond and can now draw harmonious energy into your life. It does allow you insight into the potential possible with a person of interest. You can expect many blessings to emerge from developing this situation. This is the person who takes you towards growth, kinship, and happiness. The sparks are promising with this one. Information is revealed soon, which provides you with valuable insight into this individual. Your personal life is headed towards transformation, it does allow you to embark on a new chapter of potential. Beginning to develop this situation restores a sense of balance in your life, it will enable you to remove old blockages, release outworn energy, and shine brightly with one who captures your interest.

The Aries in a relationship is given the courage to open your heart to this person. Surrendering and allowing the universe to provide you with sufficient insight, enables you to harness the power of your intuition, and correctly plot a course towards the development of feelings. This person is motivated and focused on creating a situation which offers a path towards happiness. This is a situation which tempts you to throw caution to the wind and take a leap of faith into the unknown. This is someone who you develop a deeper bond with. The timing is tricky, but it does suggest this person brings balance back to your romantic life. It is an alliance which grows stronger through the sharing of experiences together. It does lead to sunshine in your world and puts long-term plans front and center in your mind. You discover you have a great deal in common with your love interest. You develop potential with someone who stimulates your mind. This person strikes a chord for you, it feels like it is a connection worthy of your time. It enables you to broaden your horizons most spectacularly. This connection is one which involves your mind, body, and spirit. A sultry soulmate who ignites the passions within. There are chemistry and attraction to this person.

IDEAS & CREATIVITY

December is a month which provides you with creativity which is dynamic, bold, and innovative. This allows you to be a source of inspiration, you come up with original new concepts. The flow of creative energy around you is unique, pioneering, and enterprising. You feel inspired and enthusiastic about designing new proposals to develop next year. Setting your sights on specific goals provides you with a high degree of accuracy and confidence. This energy is expressed is dazzling and audacious, leading to ideas which are expansive. Your energy is original, vital, and intensely creative this month. You doing your best to nurture and support your creative side, it is a month for new growth, heightened conception, and creative fertility. By becoming a channel for artistic and creative expression, you come up with incredible plans and ideas to explore. The creativity you display this month is spontaneous, energized, and abundant.

ISSUES & HURDLES

This is a time of transformation and change in your life. Your beliefs will be challenged shortly. What you thought was so may not be so any longer. What you thought yesterday to be true may not be so tomorrow. This is a way of encouring you to be flexible. Be open to new information, this guides you to create change in your life, and it does represent a time of overcoming hurdles to achieve greater stability and growth for the future. You may be faced with change, yet this is to develop your life in a way that better suit your needs. Creativity and inspired thinking are heightened during this process, allowing you to think outside of the box., Allow yourself to surrender to the journey, and accept the flow of your destiny with grace, vision, and trust. Letting go of the cliff, sees that you fly.

The December 22nd Solstice bring an opportunity for healing. You are a highly empathetic and compassionate sentient being and struggle with the essences of pain you see in the world around you. This can be agitating to your spirit, and you need to take the time to calm, balance, and realign yourself with the gentle and simple pleasures of life. Take time to ground and stabilize your energy by engaging in acts of genourousitiy and b eing of service, be the light you wish to see in the world and this will bring you back to a place of harmony.

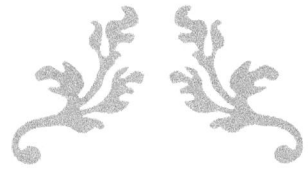

ASTROLOGICAL DIARY

2020

Astrological Diary

2020

Time is set to Coordinated Universal Time Zone (UT±0)

January

Mon 30

Tues 31

Wed 1
New Year's Day

Thurs 2

January

Fri 3
First Quarter Moon in Aries. 4.45 UTC
Quadrantids Meteor Shower. Jan 1st-5th. Peaks night of Jan 3rd.

Sat 4

Sun 5

Notes
Lucky Numbers: 11, 62, 12, 61, 32, 5
Astrological Energy: Experiential
Color: White

January

Mon 6

Tues 7

Wed 8

Thurs 9

January

Fri 10

Full Moon in Cancer. Wolf Moon. 19:21 UTC
Penumbral Lunar Eclipse.

Sat 11

Sun 12

Notes

Lucky Numbers: 23, 30, 22, 15, 27, 11
Astrological Energy: Directed
Color: Bone

January

Mon 13

Tues 14

Wed 15

Thurs 16

January

Fri 17

Last Quarter Moon in Libra. 12.58 UTC

Sat 18

Sun 19

Notes

Lucky Numbers: 32, 88, 26, 40, 92, 85
Astrological Energy: Optimistic
Color: Sky Blue

January

Mon 20
Martin Luther King Day

Tues 21

Wed 22

Thurs 23

January

Fri 24

New Moon in Capricorn. 21:42 UTC

Sat 25

Chinese New Year (Rat)

Sun 26

Last Quarter Moon in Scorpio. 21.10 UTC

Notes

Lucky Numbers: 27, 95, 10, 77, 23, 2
Astrological Energy: Visionary
Color: Indigo

January

Mon 27

Tues 28

Weds 29

Thurs 30

January/February

Fri 31

Sat 1
Imbolc

Sun 2
First Quarter Moon in Taurus. 1.42 UTC.
Groundhog Day

Notes
Lucky Numbers: 80, 11, 88, 22, 68, 99
Astrological Energy: Influential
Color: Violet

February

Mon 3

Tues 4

Weds 5

Thurs 6

February

Fri 7

Sat 8

Sun 9
Full Moon in Leo, Supermoon. Snow Moon. 7:33 UTC

Notes
Lucky Numbers: 31, 16, 96, 44, 21, 26
Astrological Energy: Commanding
Color: Midnight Blue

February

Mon 10
Mercury at largest Eastern Elongation.

Tues 11

Weds 12

Thurs 13

February

Fri 14
Valentine's Day

Sat 15
Last Quarter Moon in Scorpio. 22.17 UTC

Sun 16

Notes
Lucky Numbers: 93, 70, 24, 17, 39, 52
Astrological Energy: Imaginative
Color: Royal Blue

February

Mon 17
Presidents' Day

Tues 18
Mercury Retrograde begins

Weds 19

Thurs 20

February

Fri 21

Sat 22

Sun 23

New Moon in Aquarius. 15:32 UTC

Notes

Lucky Numbers: 49, 52, 8, 43, 85, 76
Astrological Energy: Adventurous
Color: Gold

February

Mon 24

Tues 25
Shrove Tuesday (Mardi Gras)

Weds 26
Ash Wednesday

Thurs 27

February/March

Fri 28

Sat 29

Sun 1

Notes

Lucky Numbers: 24, 67, 64, 94, 96, 55
Astrological Energy: Vivacious
Color: Yellow

March

Mon 2
First Quarter Moon in Gemini. 19.57 UTC

Tues 3

Weds 4

Thurs 5

March

Fri 6

Sat 7

Sun 8

Notes

Lucky Numbers: 84, 50, 93, 9, 48, 8
Astrological Energy: Productive
Color: Hot Pink

March

Mon 9
Full Moon in Virgo, Supermoon. Worm Moon. 17:48 UTC
Mercury Retrograde ends.
Purim (begins at sundown)

Tues 10
Purim (ends at sundown)

Weds 11

Thurs 12

March

Fri 13

Sat 14

Sun 15

Notes

Lucky Numbers: 27, 62, 37, 49, 90, 69
Astrological Energy: Passionate
Color: Cyan

March

Mon 16

Last Quarter Moon in Sagittarius. 9.34 UTC

Tues 17

St Patrick's Day

Wed 18

Thurs 19

March

Fri 20

Ostara/Spring Equinox. 3:50 UTC

Sat 21

Sun 22

Notes

Lucky Numbers: 74, 38, 95, 88, 2, 72
Astrological Energy: Constructive
Color: Spring Green

March

Mon 23

Tues 24
Mercury at most substantial Western Elongation.
Venus at most substantial Eastern Elongation.
New Moon in Aries. 9:28 UTC

Weds 25

Thurs 26

March

Fri 27

Sat 28

Sun 29

Notes

Lucky Numbers: 3, 93, 58, 91, 27, 81
Astrological Energy: Trusting
Color: Rose

March/April

Mon 30

Tues 31

Weds 1

First Quarter Moon in Cancer. 10.21 UTC
All Fools/April Fools Day

Thurs 2

April

Fri 3

Sat 4

Sun 5
Palm Sunday

Notes
Lucky Numbers: 3, 66, 5, 74, 53, 82
Astrological Energy: Celebratory
Color: Lemon

April

Mon 6

Tues 7

Weds 8
Full Moon in Libra, Supermoon. Pink Moon. 2:35 UTC
Passover (begins at sunset)

Thurs 9

April

Fri 10
Good Friday

Sat 11

Sun 12
Easter Sunday

Notes
Lucky Numbers: 86, 33, 34, 35, 75, 61
Astrological Energy: Harmonious
Color: Amber

April

Mon 13

Tues 14
Last Quarter Moon in Capricorn. 22.56 UTC

Weds 15

Thurs 16
Passover ends

April

Fri 17
Orthodox Good Friday

Sat 18

Sun 19
Orthodox Easter

Notes
Lucky Numbers: 37, 65, 90, 62, 99, 5
Astrological Energy: Inspiring
Color: Baby Blue

April

Mon 20

Tues 21

Weds 22

Lyrids Meteor Shower. April 16th-25th. Peaks night of April 22nd.
Earth Day

Thurs 23

New Moon in Taurus. 2:26 UTC
Ramadan Begins

April

Fri 24

Sat 25

Sun 26

Notes
Lucky Numbers: 88, 39, 83, 85, 26, 28
Astrological Energy: Committed
Color: Honeydew

April

Mon 27

Tues 28

Weds 29

Thurs 30
First Quarter Moon in Leo. 20.38 UTC

May

Fri 1
Beltane/May Day

Sat 2

Sun 3

Notes
Lucky Numbers: 18, 15, 51, 13, 41, 1
Astrological Energy: Complex
Color: Deep Pink

May

Mon 4

Tues 5

Weds 6
Eta Aquarids Meteor Shower. April 19th - May 28th. Peaks night of May 6th.

Thurs 7
Full Moon in Scorpio, Supermoon. Flower Moon. 10:45 UTC

May

Fri 8

Sat 9

Sun 10
Mother's Day

Notes
Lucky Numbers: 43, 65, 59, 5, 54, 34
Astrological Energy: Productive
Color: Forest Green

May

Mon 11

Tues 12

Weds 13

Thurs 14
Last Quarter Moon in Aquarius. 14.03 UTC

May

Fri 15

Sat 16

Sun 17

Notes

Lucky Numbers: 11, 68, 9, 39, 20, 88
Astrological Energy: Vibrant
Color: Aqua

May

Mon 18
Victoria Day (Canada)

Tues 19

Weds 20

Thurs 21

May

Fri 22
New Moon in Taurus. 17:39 UTC

Sat 23
Ramadan Ends

Sun 24

Notes
Lucky Numbers: 81, 34, 21, 97, 66, 43
Astrological Energy: Courageous
Color: Dark Violet

May

Mon 25
Memorial Day

Tues 26

Weds 27

Thurs 28
Shavuot (begins at sunset)

May

Fri 29

Sat 30

First Quarter Moon in Virgo. 3.30 UTC
Shavuot (ends at sunset)

Sun 31

Notes

Lucky Numbers: 29, 85, 92, 91, 60, 30
Astrological Energy: Complex
Color: Slate Blue

June

Mon 1

Tues 2

Weds 3

Thurs 4
Mercury at Greatest Eastern Elongation.

June

Fri 5
Full Moon in Sagittarius. Strawberry Moon. 19:12 UTC
Penumbral Lunar Eclipse.

Sat 6

Sun 7

Notes
Lucky Numbers: 74, 57, 56, 75, 67, 33
Astrological Energy: Daring
Color: Straw

June

Mon 8

Tues 9

Weds 10
Jupiter at Opposition.

Thurs 11

June

Fri 12

Sat 13
Last Quarter Moon in Pisces. 6.24 UTC

Sun 14
Flag Day

Notes
Lucky Numbers: 24, 61, 96, 42, 88, 47
Astrological Energy: Active
Color: Fire Brick

June

Mon 15

Tues 16

Weds 17
Mercury Retrograde begins.

Thurs 18

June

Fri 19

Sat 20

Sun 21
New Moon in Cancer. 6:41 UTC
Midsummer/Litha Solstice. 21:44 UTC
Annual Solar Eclipse.
Father's Day

Notes
Lucky Numbers: 21, 96, 92, 61, 36, 70
Astrological Energy: Exciting
Color: Cornflower Blue

June

Mon 22

Tues 23

Weds 24

Thurs 25

June

Fri 26

Sat 27

Sun 28
First Quarter Moon in Libra. 8.16 UTC

Notes
Lucky Numbers: 5, 91, 69, 39, 64, 6
Astrological Energy: Creative
Color: Red

June/July

Mon 29

Tues 30

Weds 1
Canada Day

Thurs 2

July

Fri 3

Independence Day (observed)

Sat 4

Independence Day

Sun 5

Full Moon in Capricorn. Buck Moon 4:44 UTC
Penumbral Lunar Eclipse.

Notes

Lucky Numbers: 58, 40, 99, 95, 18, 92
Astrological Energy: Curious
Color: Orange

July

Mon 6

Tues 7

Weds 8

Thurs 9

July

Fri 10

Sat 11

Sun 12

Last Quarter Moon in Aries. 23.29 UTC
Mercury Retrograde ends.

Notes

Lucky Numbers: 7, 36, 2, 20, 98 77
Astrological Energy: Stimulating
Color: Crimson

July

Mon 13

Tues 14
Jupiter at Opposition.

Weds 15

Thurs 16

July

Fri 17

Sat 18

Sun 19

Notes

Lucky Numbers: 82, 42, 66, 87, 42, 58
Astrological Energy: Inventive
Color: Ruby

July

Mon 20
New Moon in Cancer. 17:33 UTC
Saturn at Opposition.

Tues 21

Weds 22
Mercury at Greatest Western Elongation.

Thurs 23

July

Fri 24

Sat 25

Sun 26

Notes

Lucky Numbers: 31, 46, 25, 23, 43, 37
Astrological Energy: Methodical
Color: Peach

July/August

Mon 27

First Quarter Moon in Scorpio. 12.32 UTC

Tues 28

Delta Aquarids Meteor Shower. July 12th – Aug 23rd. Peaks night of July 28th.

Weds 29

Thurs 30

July/August

Fri 31

Sat 1
Lammas/Lughnasadh

Sun 2

Notes
Lucky Numbers: 35, 1, 7, 53, 26, 51
Astrological Energy: Constructive
Color: Lavender

August

Mon 3
Full Moon in Aquarius. Sturgeon Moon. 15:59 UTC

Tue 4

Wed 5

Thurs 6

August

Fri 7

Sat 8

Sun 9

Notes

Lucky Numbers: 30, 76, 90, 8, 41, 21
Astrological Energy: Independent
Color: Scarlet

August

Mon 10

Tues 11
Last Quarter Moon in Taurus. 16.45 UTC.

Weds 12
Perseids Meteor Shower. July 17th to August 24th. Peaks night of Aug 12th.

Thurs 13
Venus at Greatest Western Elongation.

August

Fri 14

Sat 15

Sun 16

Notes

Lucky Numbers: 65, 36, 98, 86, 47, 9
Astrological Energy: Aware
Color: Bronze

August

Mon 17

Tues 18

Weds 19
New Moon in Leo. 2:41 UTC

Thurs 20
Islamic New Year

August

Fri 21

Sat 22

Sun 23

Notes

Lucky Numbers: 40, 33, 63, 37, 45, 56
Astrological Energy: Spirited
Color: Mint

August

Mon 24

Tues 25
First Quarter Moon in Scorpio. 17.58 UTC

Weds 26

Thurs 27

August

Fri 28

Sat 29

Sun 30

Notes

Lucky Numbers: 22, 1, 30, 25, 2, 6
Astrological Energy: Enchanting
Color: Turquoise

August/September

Mon 31

Tues 1

Weds 2
Full Moon in Pisces. Full Corn Moon. 5:22 UTC

Thurs 3

September

Fri 4

Sat 5

Sun 6

Notes

Lucky Numbers: 86, 69, 78, 50, 71, 80
Astrological Energy: Unique
Color: Topaz

September

Mon 7
Labor Day

Tues 8

Weds 9

Thurs 10
Last Quarter Moon in Gemini. 9.26 UTC

September

Fri 11

Neptune at Opposition.

Sat 12

Sun 13

Notes

Lucky Numbers: 10, 12, 38, 62, 13, 91
Astrological Energy: Magnetic
Color: Coral

September

Mon 14

Tues 15

Weds 16

Thurs 17
New Moon in Virgo. 11:00 UTC

September

Fri 18
Rosh Hashanah (begins at sunset)

Sat 19

Sun 20
Rosh Hashanah (ends at sunset)

Notes
Lucky Numbers: 1, 54, 36, 80, 79, 57
Astrological Energy: Open
Color: White

September

Mon 21
International Day of Peace

Tues 22
Mabon/Fall Equinox. 13:31 UTC

Weds 23

Thurs 24
First Quarter Moon in Capricorn. 1.55 UTC

September

Fri 25

Sat 26

Sun 27
Yom Kippur (begins at sunset)

Notes
Lucky Numbers: 53, 89, 92, 97, 79, 71
Astrological Energy: Magical
Color: Maroon

September/October

Mon 28
Yom Kippur (ends at sunset)

Tues 29

Weds 30

Thurs 1
Full Moon in Aries. Harvest Moon. 21:05 UTC
Mercury at Greatest Eastern Elongation.

October

Fri 2
Sukkot (begins at sunset)

Sat 3

Sun 4

Notes
Lucky Numbers: 42, 11, 26, 5, 82, 14
Astrological Energy: Empathic
Color: Dark Orange

October

Mon 5

Tues 6

Weds 7

Draconids Meteor Shower. Oct 6th-10th. Peak night of Oct 7th.

Thurs 8

October

Fri 9
Sukkot (ends at sunset)

Sat 10
Last Quarter Moon in Cancer. 0.39 UTC

Sun 11

Notes
Lucky Numbers: 64, 1, 59, 48, 36, 61
Astrological Energy: Organized
Color: Chocolate

October

Mon 12
Columbus Day
Thanksgiving Day (Canada)
Indigenous People's Day

Tues 13
Mercury Retrograde begins.

Weds 14

Thurs 15

October

Fri 16

New Moon in Libra. 19:31 UTC

Sat 17

Sun 18

Notes

Lucky Numbers: 49, 37, 22, 78, 8, 4
Astrological Energy: Perceptive
Color: Salmon

October

Mon 19

Tues 20

Weds 21

Orionids Meteor Shower. Oct 2nd - Nov 7th. Peaks night of Nov 21st.

Thurs 22

October

Fri 23

First Quarter Moon in Capricorn. 13.23 UTC

Sat 24

Sun 25

Notes

Lucky Numbers: 96, 91, 20, 27, 33, 76
Astrological Energy: Mysterious
Color: Black

October

Mon 26

Tues 27

Weds 28

Thurs 29

October/November

Fri 30

Sat 31
Full Moon, Blue Moon in Taurus. Hunters Moon. 14:49 UTC
Uranus at Opposition.
Samhain/Halloween.

Sun 1
All Saints' Day

Notes
Lucky Numbers: 50, 44, 49, 97, 25, 1
Astrological Energy: Psychic
Color: Midnight

November

Mon 2

Tues 3
Mercury Retrograde ends.

Weds 4
Taurids Meteor Shower. Sept 7th - Dec 10th. Peaks on Nov 4th.

Thurs 5

November

Fri 6

Sat 7

Sun 8

Last Quarter Moon in Leo. 13.46 UTC

Notes

Lucky Numbers: 43, 18, 73, 51, 54, 92
Astrological Energy: Profound
Color: Royal Blue

November

Mon 9

Tues 10

Weds 11
Remembrance Day (Canada)
Veterans Day

Thurs 12

November

Fri 13

Sat 14

Sun 15

New Moon in Scorpio. 5:07 UTC

Notes

Lucky Numbers: 10, 7, 54, 57, 91, 21
Astrological Energy: Hectic
Color: Teal

November

Mon 16

Tues 17

Leonids Meteor Shower. Nov 6th-30th. Peaks night of Nov 17th.

Weds 18

Thurs 19

November

Fri 20

Sat 21

Sun 22
First Quarter Moon in Pisces. 4.45 UTC

Notes
Lucky Numbers: 75, 92, 5, 47, 99, 93
Astrological Energy: Structured
Color: Sky Blue

November

Mon 23

Tues 24

Weds 25

Thurs 26
Thanksgiving Day (US)

November

Fri 27

Sat 28

Sun 29

Notes

Lucky Numbers: 7, 25, 52, 75, 67, 55
Astrological Energy: Social
Color: Magenta

November/December

Mon 30
Full Moon in Gemini. Beaver Moon. 9:30 UTC
Penumbral Lunar Eclipse.

Tues 1

Weds 2

Thurs 3

December

Fri 4

Sat 5

Sun 6

Notes

Lucky Numbers: 87, 3, 92, 14, 83, 13
Astrological Energy: Impulsive
Color: Midnight Blue

December

Mon 7

Tues 8
Last Quarter Moon in Virgo. 0.37 UTC

Weds 9

Thurs 10
Hanukkah (begins at sunset)

December

Fri 11

Sat 12

Sun 13

Geminids Meteor Shower. Dec 7th-17th. Peaks nights of Dec 13th-15th.

Notes

Lucky Numbers: 67, 10, 7, 43, 76, 99
Astrological Energy: Vibrant
Color: Snow

December

Mon 14

New Moon in Sagittarius. 16:17 UTC

Tues 15

Weds 16

Thurs 17

December

Fri 18

Hanukkah (ends at sunset)

Sat 19

Sun 20

Notes

Lucky Numbers: 16, 85, 10, 96, 67, 1
Astrological Energy: Festive
Color: Powder Blue

December

Mon 21

Ursids Meteor Shower. Dec 17th – 25th. Peaks night of Dec 21st.
Great Conjunction of Jupiter and Saturn.
Yule/ Winter Solstice. 10:02 UTC
First Quarter Moon in Pisces. 23.41 UTC

Tues 22

Weds 23

Thurs 24

December

Fri 25
Christmas Day

Sat 26
Boxing Day (Canada & Uk)
Kwanzaa begins

Sun 27

Notes
Lucky Numbers: 33, 6, 30, 17, 80, 76
Astrological Energy: Graceful
Color: White

December

Mon 28

Tues 29

Weds 30
Full Moon in Cancer. Cold Moon. 3:28 UTC

Thurs 31
New Year's Eve

January

Fri 1
New Year's Day
Kwanzaa ends

Sat 2

Sun 3

Notes
Lucky Numbers: 23, 15, 12, 29, 71, 86
Astrological Energy: Aware
Color: Green Yellow

May the stars shine brightly in your world in 2020, and beyond.

About Crystal Sky

Crystal is passionate about the universe, helping others, and personal development. Crystal produces a range of astrologically minded diaries to celebrate the universal forces which affect us all. All reviews are read and appreciated.

Other Titles in the 2020 range:

Fairy Moon Diary 2020: Fairy Messages & Astrological Datebook
Shaman Moon Diary 2020: Shamanic Messages & Astrological Datebook

When not writing about the stars, you can find Crystal under them, gazing up at the abundance that surrounds us all, with her dog by her side.

www.ingramcontent.com/pod-product-compliance
Lightning Source LLC
Chambersburg PA
CBHW051801040426
42446CB00007B/462